YouTube Grow

GW00857329

How to Drive Massive Traffic ......nel And
Turn People Into Rabid Fans

By Jeff Abston

YouTube Growth Hacking

Copyright ©2018 by (Jeff Abston)

ISBN-13: 978-1985089020

ISBN-10: 1985089025

Table of Contents

Who Is This Book for?

Since its emergence in the early 2000's, YouTube has seen amazing growth as a website and a platform for anyone and everyone. It is estimated that it now sees roughly 15 billion visitors a month and the company sold to Google in 2006 for 1.15 billion dollars. The site is no longer just for cats doing adorable things and parody music videos. Now YouTube can be the key to your success, either as an entertainer or business owner. Individuals have parlayed viral success into long-term careers in show business, comedians have started their careers by posting videos on the website, musicians have gained international attention by posting their music, and businesses have advertised to a younger audience by using YouTube.

The fact that YouTube is (largely) free makes for a much wider audience than some other platforms available for marketing, and it has also made the audience on YouTube the highly coveted younger demographic. Kids who have Internet access at home but not the money to spend on other viewing platforms find YouTube to be a source of hours of entertainment and they flock to videos of their favorite stars on their preferred channels. The other major source of viewers are cord-cutters who no longer want to pay for cable and satellite TV; and as more people continue to cut the cord every year due to the frustration with cable companies and, more importantly, cable bills, the number of viewers on YouTube continues to flourish.

There is extreme financial value for a small startup company marketing on the Internet, specifically YouTube. Small companies that find ways to successfully grow their online presence and run savvy marketing campaigns on sites like YouTube are able to quickly expand their business in today's digital environment.

With the many demographics of people using the free site continuously, everyone stands to gain something from having a popular YouTube channel these days. This may be why the number of channels on the site continues to climb as the number of content creators rises and more and more people are wondering how they can get noticed in a sea of videos. Certainly it is not easy to gain a substantial following on the video sharing platform anymore, but in this book the keys to building a sustained plan for success will be outlined. Make no mistake, there isn't an easy way to be successful on YouTube. As with anything, people do get lucky and find success occasionally without having to work hard, but most of the time hard work is what brings about the highest reward.

Going Viral

While it's true that hard work is the biggest key to gaining long standing success on YouTube, there is no doubt that "going viral" also has value in gaining widespread attention when it comes to your channel. Having a viral video means that you have a video that gets shared among so many people that it becomes a part of pop culture at the time and grows into something that most every person has seen or heard of. These videos get passed around from friend to friend and family member to family member until they've reached a massive number of views, often in the millions or tens of millions. Often, the channels and individuals in these videos become instant stars to the public and many become recognizable to millions almost overnight.

One important thing to note about having a video go viral, that will help you parlay a momentary bump in views into longstanding success, is that you should have the video monetized before it becomes a blockbuster. Monetizing a video means that you went through the necessary procedures on YouTube to set your channel up to make revenues from every view you accumulate. YouTube makes revenue on its videos through the ads placed at the beginning, in the middle, and the end of each one; and having your videos set up to be monetized makes it possible for you to see a portion of the revenue made from the ads on your videos. The more views your video accumulates, the more money generated through ads on it. Obviously, the video that goes viral will make a significant chunk of money in ad revenue; and if you have already set the video up to be monetized beforehand, you stand to make a lot in the wake of a viral video.

While having one video become very successful doesn't mean that you will be able to turn it into a successful channel overall, if you do gain a substantial chunk of money from that one viral video, you can then use the revenue money on things that will benefit your channel long term. Higher quality video equipment, better audio equipment, and the funds to promote your video on YouTube to gain even more eyes on your channel are the types of things you can afford with the revenue money you just made through one successful video.

Essentially, you can take the money you make from a viral video and invest it back into your channel to make sure that your channel sees long-term success. Again, having a viral video doesn't mean that you will be able to turn it into a successful channel, but if you are smart about how you use this temporary success, you may be able to turn it into permanent success.

The hardest part of this whole equation is having a video get popular to begin with. Think about all of the videos that come to mind that you remember becoming major hits. What was it about the videos that made them so popular to the point that they became temporarily ingrained in our culture? Usually, a video becomes viral if it has something rare in it, something that makes it unique and something that everyone wants to see when they hear about it. This is why having a video go truly viral is so difficult and rare, and also why you shouldn't count on this technique to build your channel. It is possible that it might happen, and if it does you should use it to your advantage, but the odds are not in your favor. No matter how great your marketing team is or how adorable your friend's cat is, the idea that one of your videos will explode overnight into a major success is unlikely and not something even needed to grow a channel into a steady platform.

If you look into many of the videos that you can think of that have gone viral, you will find that many of the channels associated with those videos are not doing well. Maybe they no longer post content or the videos they post now don't get very many views at all. It is also possible that the channel on which the video originated never saw any views from the viral video to begin with. Many videos that become hits end up being shared from a channel that didn't originally post them, but rather the videos were copied and posted to another channel, recognizing their potential for success.

That is why this form of growing your channel is probably the least effective, but it should always be mentioned as there is amazing potential that exists when one of your videos happens to reach a "viral" level of views.

Interacting With Users

It is amazing how many people forget the social aspect of social media marketing. There are countless individuals and businesses that want to grow their channel from the ground up but they never interact with other users on any social networking websites. YouTube is itself a social network, thanks to the comments section found under (most) videos and the way you are able to find other individuals and businesses in your niche with whom you can then interact. This is one of the aspects of the website that seems to be forgotten by most content creators when they are griping about how their videos never get any views. How are they supposed to if they aren't interacting with people on the website on which you are posting them?

One of the best ways to grow your channel when you don't have a lot of views is to search on YouTube for recently posted videos in areas that are similar to the kind of content your channel posts. This will bring up results by channels that also don't have a lot of viewers, at least not yet. The best thing you can do is spend a little bit of time watching one or two of their videos and give an honest and productive comment on one of them. Obviously, if you have nothing nice to say, then don't say anything at all; but if there is one or two things you noticed in the video you liked, say so.

As this channel doesn't have a lot of viewers yet, they probably don't get a ton of comments either, so the fact that you commented will definitely be noticed, unlike the huge channels where your comment could get lost in a sea of thousands of others. There is a good chance that the user will notice your comment and out of curiosity click on your channel to see what type of you have. This could lead to nothing more than one more view of one of your videos, but there is a chance they will like what they see and become a new subscriber. Maybe they will even comment back on one of your videos and you will even form a friendship and become allies on YouTube. This type of social interaction is something often lost on content creators.

Subscribe to other channels too and comment regularly if you like their videos. Find smaller channels that you actually enjoy, which means you'll want to watch their videos anyway, and then become a regular contributor to their comment section and you will get noticed fairly quickly.

While interacting with other people on their channels is hugely important to marketing your channel and achieving growth, it is also wise not to forget your own comment section and the viewers you already have. Never forget to respond to comments from users under your videos and try to do so quickly. People appreciate content creators who seem available and genuine, so try to remain available and respond politely when you can to comments. You can't make everyone happy all of the time with the content you post, but you can control how you react to people not being happy. Listen to people's concerns and comments and try to build relationships with your subscribers, which will make it less likely that they will unsubscribe when given a chance.

This is the best way to keep your content headed in the right direction. Ask your audience what they want to see in your next video or videos, and there will most definitely be a lot of requests. What you do with the requests is entirely up to you, but it is important not to ignore them or else your viewers will not feel appreciated and heard. Take their suggestions and use them to come up with ideas for the videos you will make next. This will keep your viewers feeling like they are a part of your channel more than ever and it will remind them that you are actually listening. The other positive to this is that the content you create is more likely to be well received when your viewers had a hand in creating it.

Giveaways

If you've spent much time on YouTube over the past few years, you've probably noticed that channels actively trying to grow often do events and contests for their subscribers. This is a highly effective way to get people to come to your channel while at the same time making the people already there feel appreciated. The next time you have some extra money in your marketing budget, considering buying a small, but significant, prize item that you can then randomly give away on your channel. If your channel exists in a specific niche, it would be best to obtain an item in that niche to give away as well. This will ensure that your subscribers will actually want the item you are giving away as a prize.

Running a contest or giveaway is so effective because it makes your fans feel like you care about them enough to literally give them a present. It is like telling them that you appreciate them so much that you want to give them something. It makes your subscribers feel like you are down to earth and care about them, even as your channel is potentially growing with each passing day.

A contest is also effective because of all the new potential subscribers it will attract. If the item you are giving away is significant, your current subscribers may share it with friends and family that they know would like the item. Those friends and family members will come to your channel to enter the giveaway as well, and while they are there, it is possible they will enjoy your other content and decide to stick around permanently. The sharing of your videos or channel is similar to the effect that happens when you have a video go viral, but you have much more control over when this effect occurs, as you decide when and how you want to do a contest.

The other reason contests are impactful when it comes to attracting subscribers is because there are people out there that just search for giveaways on YouTube. There are people who go on YouTube and search for the word, "contest" or "giveaway", and then look for videos where they can enter contests. Yes, these people are only interested in the prizes and may not care about your other content, but if you do contests regularly, it is still possible that they will subscribe to your channel just for those videos. This may not seem like it would help your channel overall, but isn't a new subscriber, no matter why they are subscribing, still a good thing? Of course, just like the friends and family members who are shown your channel by someone else, it is still possible that they will check out some of your other content and become a fan and a subscriber for the right reasons. You don't want giveaways and contests to take over your channel completely, but it is certainly an effective tool to give your channel a little shot of attention every now and then.

An important thing to remember with contests is to always make the contests fair for your subscribers and never a scam. If you claim that you are going to give an item away on your channel, you must actually go through with it and give that item away. You can't make fake contests and cheat people to gain attention for your channel. Beyond the obvious ethical issues, given the Internet age we live in, people will definitely find out that you scam your fans and it will result in the utter destruction of your channel and maybe your personal life as well. Always be truthful and fair when you run contests on your channel.

SEO

SEO stands for search engine optimization and it is very important for getting views on the videos you post. One of the most common ways that people find channels they subscribe to search for a topic and a particular channel comes up near the top of the results. This takes some savvy and understanding of SEO unless you are already a popular channel, as videos that have a lot of views on a topic will always appear near the top of the search results anyway. SEO is a complicated skill that is difficult to explain and there could easily be a separate entire book on the subject; but the fact that it is not an easy skill to master is exactly why those who understand it are able to gain success on YouTube. The titles for the videos you post on your channel should include key words that people will search for. It is not a good idea to make titles that abandon all creative integrity just for the sake of SEO, but whenever you are creating titles for videos, it should be kept in mind that whenever possible, common words often searched for on YouTube should be included.

Also, making your titles exciting is an important part of SEO. When people search for the keywords included in your title, they should want to click on your video because it is something they want to see. Maybe selling yourself or your videos as thrilling isn't something you are good at, whether it be because you are too shy or humble or both, but selling your videos is a major part of growing your channel. So make the titles contain keywords that sound exciting.

The other major aspect of search engine optimization is how you tag your videos. Tags are keywords you attach to your video so that YouTube knows what exactly is in your video and what categories falls under. Knowing how to properly tag your videos is one of the most important things involved with posting videos that will get the right people to see them. Let's say you have a YouTube channel all about birds and you want other people who love birds to find your videos. The best way to make this happen is by adding tags to your videos that include keywords that bird lovers would be searching for on YouTube. Obviously, it is best to only put tags that specifically relate to your videos, whatever niche they may be in, because this will get all the people who enjoy that niche to find them, but there are SEO tricks that will generate more widespread views if you don't mind using them.

When you understand the current trends and popular current events in the world you have a better chance of adding the keywords that will attract major views.

Understanding that a major incident happening at the time, such as an election or a weather event, could be used in the tags (if added cunningly enough) to bring in some of the many people searching for related videos, is a more intermediate level of SEO skill. While typically marketing involves promoting your channel actively, using proper SEO skills in relation to the tags on your videos is more of a passive technique to gain views and accumulate possible subscribers. These tags are constantly working in the background of your videos to bring your videos up in search results. This is why SEO is so crucial to gaining a following on YouTube and growing your channel. You can only work so many hours every day to build your channel on YouTube, but well-picked tags can work 24 hours a day and 7 days a week to generate more clicks and more eyes on your videos.

Thumbnails That Pop

One of the most obvious and noticeable things you may need to work on when it comes to your videos is the quality of your thumbnails. A thumbnail refers to the small picture shown when your videos comes up in a search result or are listed anywhere on YouTube's website. It may show a random point in the video itself or it can be a picture you upload that has words describing more of what happens. While you may not want to spend all the time it can take to create a really impressive looking thumbnail, it should be noted how important it is to getting many views on any video. Other than possibly the video title, the thumbnail that represents your video is the first thing people see when your video pops up in a search result or in the recommended videos section. The quality, or lack thereof, can make or break whether or not someone actually clicks on the video to view it. How many times have you searched for a topic on YouTube and scrolled through the results, peering at the tiny thumbnails present for every video and judging each one based on the quality of the picture shown. Even if a video has a perfect title that is exactly what the user is looking for, it is very possible that they will pass up the video if the thumbnails are of a low quality or seem to be about something different than the title indicates. When you look at some of the most popular channels on YouTube, both individual and professional, you will notice that most of the top channels have very clean and professional quality thumbnails.

It is recommended that you use a picture editor to create thumbnails that pop and will draw a user's attention. While there are many picture editors on the market for whom you have to pay money, and they probably offer more value and give you more options to work with, it is not necessary to pay anything to make a solid thumbnail. Free editors like Pixlr can do the trick just fine and will accomplish what you need. The key to a great thumbnail is making it work in unison with your title in such a way that will make users feel they have to view your video because it contains something amazing or unique. Make the font of the words you put on the thumbnail look clean and modern. Make the words you use on the thumbnail provocative and exciting. Also, use a picture of high quality, a high definition shot in good focus that users will understand easily on any device. While your thumbnail may look good on your home or office PC, you must remember that many users view YouTube on their phones and tablets these days and the picture may be significantly smaller on their screen. On some devices, the thumbnails are actually more important than the titles, such as on phones, because the titles are often cut off due to a lack of space on the screen, but the picture is still viewable clearly and in full.

Sometimes content creators try to make thumbnails to up the quality on their channel but actually end up hurting more than helping themselves. They do this by making some common mistakes that should be avoided at all costs if you want to find success on YouTube. Many times, creators will use Microsoft Paint to create their thumbnails and this is not a good idea. While free picture editors can do the trick of creating a great thumbnail, Paint really does not have the capability of making a professional-looking picture. Besides, everyone can typically tell that you used MS Paint and this takes away from the quality of the picture. YouTube can be compared to a magic show, in that if users know the secret to all of your tricks, it kind of ruins it for them. You should be doing such a good job at creating content that they don't really know how you do it.

Another mistake people make when creating a thumbnail is when they use a picture that is a poor quality. If anyone has a hard time understanding what is happening in your thumbnail, then you didn't do the picture correctly. The picture should be clear, in focus and of a high pixel quality. The picture should be zoomed in enough such that a user doesn't have to squint or strain their eyes to understand what they are looking at. You are trying to make content that is easily digestible and starts with the presentation of your videos thumbnails.

Another mistake people make is using a picture completely unrelated to the video's content. While this may result in more clicks if the picture's content is salacious enough, it typically won't result in more long-term fans and subscribers. People will realize that you are using an unrelated thumbnail to attract cheap views and they quickly become tired and upset at what you are doing. Remember, half the battle is getting them to watch the video, but the other half is getting them to want to see more after they have viewed it.

Don't Stop, Collaborate and Listen

This section goes back to the social network aspect of YouTube mentioned earlier. Collaborating with other YouTube channels is a great way to gain some new fans and grow your channel. Not only that, but you also continue to make sure that the content on your channel doesn't get stale when you work with other channels. The YouTube personalities or companies with whom you collaborate will bring their own flavor to your videos and add a new element previously not there. However, unless you are considering a complete merger of two channels, you want to keep collaboration videos to a minimum, as fans of your channel are already subscribed to your channel for what you currently offer as a standalone channel, and you don't want to alienate them.

The biggest benefit of collaborating with other channels is the exposure your channel will receive from the audience of the other channel with which you do a video or multiple videos. This is a huge opportunity to gain new subscribers to your channel as you attempt to grow. Everyone already subscribed to the other YouTube content creator's channel will instantly be exposed to your videos, and if they like what they see, they may very well subscribe to your channel. This concept is similar to the idea behind crossover episodes of television shows or being a guest on a late night talk show. Putting your channel in front of new eyes is always a good thing and will contribute to the growth of your channel. The main thing to remember is that you should collaborate with other channels in the same niche as yours. For example, if your channel is related to the sport of golf, then you should collaborate with other golf-related channels. This is the kind of collaboration that leads to new subscribers. If you are collaborating with channels that make content completely different from yours, it still may result in new subscribers, but the chances are much lower. Both you and the people you consider working with should understand your niche and know whether or not it is a good idea for both of your channels to work together or not.

The other reason it's good to collaborate with others is because it *may* lead to something great where the two of your channels work so well together that you want to work together long-term, possibly in some sort of merger. This is like when a great band finally finds the perfect combination of people on each instrument and starts creating musical masterpieces. It would be foolish to disregard a great combination of two channels and go your separate ways if you both work together really well. In such cases, you could join forces permanently and you would have an ally in your attempt to grow on YouTube. In the highly competitive world of the Internet, it is good to have someone to work with and help you on your way to a successful channel. Certainly, don't ignore once-in-a lifetime opportunities just because you think the growth of your channel should be done solely on your own. One thing to always remember in marketing is to seize every opportunity for exposure and success.

Collaborating with other channels should also remind you not to get too egotistical and competitive on YouTube. When you are working with another channel, it means you want that other channel to continue to succeed. It is important to remember that all other channels don't have to fail for you to succeed. Other people's success should be celebrated just as much as your own. Don't forget to stay grounded, and your subscribers will notice that you are still down to earth and appreciate you for it.

Always make sure when you collaborate that the videos on the channel where you make an appearance allow you to plug your own channel. Then ask the other person to post links in the description of the video that go on your channel. It does little good to collaborate with another person for exposure if you don't make it easy for their subscribers to get to your content if they like what they see. The amount of effort people are willing to exert on the Internet is minimal and fleeting. Sometimes, the least bit of effort to get to your content can stop someone from ever seeing your videos. Make it clear where they can find you and put your channel an easy click away, and you will certainly see new subscribers rolling in.

Be Consistent

There is a reason why television shows generally stick to a schedule of a new episode every week at the same time and on the same night. This is because people easily lose interest in what you have to offer if you don't post content on a regular basis. When was the last time you liked a channel on YouTube but then after you subscribed, you found that you had a problem with the way they posted videos? Typically, people don't like channels that post very sporadically. This doesn't mean you have to force a schedule on yourself that is too strenuous. The frequency at which you post can be anything from once a day to once a month, but whatever you decide, you should stick to it and post on that schedule consistently. Imagine if a show on television aired an episode on a Wednesday night and then a month later aired another episode on a Monday night, and then a week later aired on a Thursday. You would probably be pretty annoyed with the schedule constantly changing and more than likely give up on trying to watch it, unless the show was really amazing. The same thing applies to channels on YouTube. You can't expect to grow your audience if they never know when or if you will post new content. If you don't post in a long time, for all they know you will never be posting again and they will just go ahead and unsubscribe. This routinely happens to newer channels on YouTube and it stunts their growth significantly. Be disciplined and you will reap rewards.

Again, you don't have to force a difficult schedule on yourself but pick one that suits you best. If you don't think you can put out one video a day, then make it one per week. It is also a good idea to let your audience know when they can expect more videos, so that they will look for them to be posted. This is similar to commercials on TV that promote new episodes of shows that will air. The network lets everyone know when they will be airing so that the most people possible watch. Letting your audience know when new episodes will air can backfire tremendously, however, if you happen not to stick to your schedule. Imagine if FOX told everyone a new episode of The Simpsons will air at a specific time and then when everyone tunes in to watch, there is no new episode at all. The network gives no explanation and just says that it will air next week. How would fans of the show feel and would they bother to tune in next week possibly getting burned again? Probably not. Everyone would be upset and it would make FOX look terrible and unprofessional. This is why if you tell your subscribers when new videos will post, you stick to that schedule. While YouTube videos are free to watch, people still feel like they are getting cheated if you don't post videos when you say you will and are inconsistent.

Posting content regularly keeps you fresh in the minds of your subscribers and will keep them feeling like they have a relationship with your channel. Your videos can become a part of their routine and will become integrated into their way of life. If your videos are created correctly, after each video, people will be left wanting more of your channel; and this feeling can be capitalized on only if you are posting content regularly.

Quality vs. Quantity

This ties into the last section about picking a posting schedule that you are comfortable with. You also have to select a schedule that adheres to the decision you make as far as quality versus quantity goes. This means that you have to decide if you would like to post videos less often with videos having a higher quality content, or if you would rather post videos more often with a lower quality content. Each side has its good and bad points.

If you think that posting content very often is the most important thing to do with your channel, than you can opt for the quantity route. This is a good technique to keep your channel growing on YouTube, as you will consistently have videos that will show up on the recently added section of the site. People that happened to search for recently uploaded videos will have a better chance of finding your channel if you are uploading often. This is also good because in the heavily populated site of YouTube, it can be hard to get noticed; and one way is to attempt to flood the site with your content. The more videos you put out, the better chance people will notice you and your channel. This is an issue of mere statistics. The downside of posting content very frequently is that inevitably the content of your videos will suffer in quality. You won't have as much time to work on each one you put out and the quality will be significantly lower, unless you have the resources to hire a team to work for your channel and keep the quality high. You may end up feeling trapped by your video schedule and resent the feeling that you don't have time to do some of the things you want to do with your content. Some viewers will be put off by your channel if you don't have a high quality production and content, while others won't care at all and just want more.

On the other hand, if you choose to focus on quality instead of quantity, your videos will be highly professional and have strong content value. There is less of a chance of filler content or wasted time and people will likely be impressed with any video they see. You have more options as far as creative content goes, because you have more time to work on each video and experiment. Overall, each video will be more impressive but there is a downside to this tactic as well. If you are posting videos less often and focusing on making each exceptional, then you won't be flooding YouTube with your content making it more difficult for people to find you. Think about how certain commercials on television are run constantly seemingly on every channel, to the point where whatever that commercial is selling, everyone knows about it. You want to do this on YouTube with your channel, if possible by focusing on quality over quantity.

In the end only you can decide which direction to take for your channel. Each side has its pros and cons, and both tactics have been used to create successful channels in the past that have grown beyond all expectations. The most important thing to remember when it comes to making this decision is what the purpose of your channel is to begin with. If you are an individual who just wants to create things and make something they are proud of, then maybe you should choose quality. If you are running a YouTube channel for business and the main purpose is to grow your channel to help it, then perhaps quantity is the better option. Either way, it is a good idea to decide which direction before you start posting too much content and gaining subscribers. Each subscriber has different preferences for the type of channels they view and if you change directions suddenly, they may become unhappy and want to stop watching your channel, stunting your growth in the process.

Be Professional

No matter the speed at which you are creating videos and putting them out, you should always remember to make them look as professional as possible. Make videos that are streamed at high definition, at least 720p resolution. Create intros and outros that are clean and professional-looking. Once again, make thumbnails that look eye-popping and professional. It is a good idea to have channel branding that looks modern as well. This means adding a logo to each thumbnail or a watermark to each video. A unified color scheme for your channel makes everything look like you know what you are doing and that you take YouTube seriously.

The biggest part of looking professional is definitely the resolution of your videos. People today can access and stream YouTube videos on their television sets through smart TVs and streaming devices. Now more than ever, if you have grainy or low resolution videos on your channel, people will notice and it can make those who would otherwise subscribe to your channel go somewhere else. It is not 2005 anymore and people don't expect your videos to look like they were shot then either. A good bar to set for yourself is to strive to make your channel look like something on TV.

Obviously, you don't have hundreds of thousands of dollars (probably) to spend on making your channel look professional, but it is key that you attempt to make them look as close to something on television as possible. This is the level of quality people expect, even with YouTube channels, and this will maximize your possible viewer base. Utilizing free or cheap production equipment that still offers high quality results, you can easily achieve very professional content without breaking the budget.

Free or cheap video editing tools, picture editing tools, and audio tools are all available online. You will need to be somewhat technically savvy, or capable of learning some technical skills in order to use them; but learning to use these tools can be invaluable to your channel moving forward. The other option available is to pay someone to handle the technical production aspects of your channel so that you don't have to worry about it yourself, but this requires that you have the budget to spend on hiring someone.

Small details, like making sure the volume of the audio in your videos is at a reasonable level can actually make or break a channel. People are not going to subscribe to channels where the volume of the videos is so low that they can barely be heard; and likewise, they will not enjoy a channel where the audio is so loud that it blows out their computer speakers.

Obviously, the audio should be crisp and clear but the volume level should be leveled out and tested on multiple devices before and after being uploaded to ensure an acceptable sound.

The editing of each video should be professional as well. This means that each video should be of a reasonable length, not too extremely long and not too short. There shouldn't be a lot of dead space that serves no purpose. If nothing is happening or being said for a full five or ten minutes, there is definitely no reason to include it. Edit your videos down in such way that cuts out any unnecessary fat and leaves only the most important and impressive parts. While, like many movie directors, you may feel that every piece of video you shot is meaningful and brilliant, put yourself in the shoes of the viewer and realize that some parts can be eliminated.

Don't Be Too Professional

Professionalism is important for making your channel look like a big deal and something worth viewing, but this shouldn't make you lose touch with reality. It is important to always stay grounded and relevant to your audience. While viewers appreciate well-produced, high quality videos, they also want the content to be relatable and fun. For instance, there are plenty of very professional business executives in the television business. These executives wear suits and look professional in every way, including their physical appearance. They also have years, sometimes decades, of experience creating well-produced and high-quality programming on television. However, most viewers today, and definitely the younger audience, will say that there is nothing that ruins a television show faster than network executives getting too involved in the production of the shows they love. To put it plainly, these executives are the perfect embodiment of professionalism but that professionalism doesn't help them relate to or understand an audience and what they want to see. It is important that no matter what level of production your channel is able to reach that you don't forget what really made you popular to begin with, and this is always going to be your content and likeability.

One of the most common criticisms of YouTube channels after they succeed is that they forget what made them popular to begin with and in a sense they sell out. While this isn't the biggest concern you need to have when your channel hasn't even become popular yet, it is important to remember when your channel does finally and hopefully takes off. Growing your channel is the first step, but you could just as easily lose all of that growth in a short amount of time if you don't remain grounded and relatable to your audience. This doesn't mean you should be unprofessional, but don't become one of the talking suits that so routinely interferes with and ruins good content in television and movies either.

Promote Your Channel

You may be thinking that this entire book is mostly about promoting your channel, and you'd be right, but promoting is actually an option on YouTube where you can spend money as well. YouTube gives everyone the option to "promote" their channel on the site. This means that you actually pay YouTube a sum of money and one or multiple of your videos will show up in special places on the website. If you've ever clicked on a video and an "ad" played beforehand, and it was more like a separate video than an ad, this was a promoted video. Promoting gives you the opportunity to have your video played before other people's videos of a related content, or shows up more commonly on recommended videos lists. It may put your video in the related videos section of other videos that aren't yours as well. Obviously, this is a really good option for spreading your channel around and gaining subscribers. There's not an easier way to promote your channel than this option. The question ultimately becomes whether the number of subscribers you gain is worth the amount of money you have to spend getting YouTube to promote your work. You have to have funds to pay for this promotion and this means having enough money budgeted in your company's marketing funds or having enough in your personal banking account to do so. If you believe the amount of fans you gain is worth the price, then it may be the best way to go.

If your YouTube channel is meant to promote your business to begin with, this is definitely a good option. Even if the promotion doesn't add that many followers to your YouTube channel, it still may add new customers to your business. This may be cheaper than running more conventional advertisement campaigns on television or other platforms. As mentioned earlier, the demographics that watch YouTube regularly are considerably younger, making advertising there a great way to attract a young and more hip customer base.

Just make sure that the content of your videos is not too controversial or inappropriate, as especially lately, YouTube has not been so keen on spreading these types of videos around their website, as it affects their advertisement options with other companies. If you have controversial content, it is still possible to promote, but it is recommended to use your least brazen videos to use this feature.

Use Your Other Media Accounts

You may not have a hugely popular YouTube channel yet, and it is perfectly fine, but do you have a few thousand followers on Twitter? How many Facebook friends do you have? It is surprising how often people tend to separate their different social media accounts, as if they can't promote one on the other. Even if you have no subscribers on YouTube, you can still share your channel and videos on your other social media accounts which will help you grow considerably faster. Twitter might be the greatest ally, as it uses the hashtag feature extremely well which will help you get your content easier to people searching for it. Post a tweet from your account every time you post a video, or use social media managing tools, like Buffer, to schedule a tweet once every few days after you post a video. Use proper and popular hashtags and make the tweet as interesting as possible. Even if you don't have a ton of followers on Twitter, you might be surprised at how much difference sharing your videos on the site can make for the amount of traffic you get to your channel.

Even if you're a business, you should have multiple social media accounts already in order to take advantage of the possible revenue growth, and hopefully these accounts have significant followings. If this is the case, then sharing your videos on the company's Twitter, Facebook, and Instagram accounts is a no-brainer and will help grow the channel a lot. If you are an individual, it may mean you don't have as much of an online presence, but that doesn't mean that the aunt you haven't seen for a couple years wouldn't click on a link to your YouTube videos if given the chance. That's why it is still important to take advantage of every social media account you have and share your videos like crazy on all of them. Well, share them a lot, but don't go overboard. Everyone will get annoyed if you are doing nothing but sharing your YouTube videos on Twitter and Facebook every five minutes. Be persistent in your advertisements, but don't let them completely take over your other accounts.

Also, if you don't have a huge following on these sites, it is recommended that you work on your growth there as well. Work on growing your presence on Twitter can be just as much work as on YouTube, even if YouTube is your main focus. If you grow on Twitter, you will have a bigger platform on which to share your videos and this will grow your YouTube channel as well. Don't look at each social media platform as a separate entity that doesn't affect any other. Look at them all as different parts of one big social media presence, so if you are successful on Facebook, it will help you be successful on YouTube. Explaining exactly how to grow your presence on each of these sites would easily fill another book, but it cannot be understated how helpful it can be to have successful social media platforms on which to share your videos when you are trying to get noticed on YouTube's densely-populated website. Trying to do everyone solely on YouTube is not recommended anymore, as the website has grown to such a large size that you would just be handicapping yourself and your channel. Not to mention that many of the same skills you will hone on other websites can help you break through on YouTube as well. This means that you will be gaining valuable experience on these other sites that can be used during your time on YouTube.

Create Content That Can be Shared

One common mistake by people with YouTube channels is that they try to imitate some of their heroes in the entertainment business and perhaps lose sight of the value of making content that can be shared with everyone. Most people watch R-rated movies and many enjoy raunchy comedies and dark dramas, but making content that pushes the boundaries on YouTube can make it more difficult when starting out. To grow your channel, it is necessary that people share your videos and your channel with a lot of friends and colleagues. The fact is that people are less likely to share your content with everyone they know if they think your videos might offend some of them. So, instead of getting your videos shared with the ten people a person knows, you might only get shared with six of the ten. While the content you're making might be exactly the kind you want to make, it is important to remember the consequences of making offensive content on the Internet.

Obviously, you may not care and want to make that kind of content for a reason. If that is your creative prerogative, then you should definitely go for it.

However, if your main goal is to make a channel that will grow quickly and easily and find an audience as soon as possible, understanding that content should not be too offensive or raunchy is important. Looking at television and understanding why most shows avoid certain topics and words is important in this case. All of the channels on cable packages don't have to censor the content played on their channels, but nearly all of them do. Why is that? This happens because the channels know that they need advertisers in order to make money, and these advertisers are less likely to pay for spots on their channels if the content is too offensive and will hurt their brand. While you may think that advertisers are not something your channel will have to deal with for a long time, and that is true when you are starting out, you should understand early that YouTube will never pay you well if advertisers don't like the content of your videos. YouTube may have to disallow ads on your videos to keep their advertisers happy and this will mean that you may never make good money on the website.

If you don't care about advertisers or ever making money on the site, that is fine and probably a good attitude to have, but there is still another reason why censoring your content is helpful in growing your channel. YouTube videos that are more family friendly tend to find an audience faster, as families with religious values will find your videos more viewer friendly than a lot of the other content on the Internet and YouTube today. There is an audience out there that doesn't like boundary-pushing content and that audience could be your first big push for your channel.

Also keep in mind the niche or subject of your videos when you are considering whether or not you should censor your videos. If you review children's toys on YouTube, you probably shouldn't curse a lot in your videos or make a ton of vulgar jokes. There is nothing entirely wrong with doing either of those things, but doing them in these types of videos will make it hard for you to find an audience. People looking up reviews of children's toys probably don't want to hear that kind of stuff in the videos they click on.

Networking in Real Life

While Internet marketing might be more important in this day and age, it doesn't mean that you should ignore the way marketing used to be. If you have a business in the real world that is profiting nicely and that sees a good amount of traffic, you could always market your YouTube channel to those people as well. For example, if you own a small store or business, you could make a sign that you would then place inside the physical establishment that points visitors to your channel. Because of the way YouTube links look, as they are randomly generated and people don't change these default links, it may not look like a link that people will remember easily. This is often true, and a major reason why people don't share their YouTube link in real life. You may find it easier and more effective to share your YouTube user or channel name with visitors instead. Rather than making a sign with your channel's link on it, you could make a sign that says the name of your channel on YouTube. That way people can remember your (hopefully) easy-to-remember and catchy username and search for you on the website later.

Real life marketing can be valuable for those who have accumulated a large network of business partners and associates through more conventional means. If you have a lot of co-workers at your job, you could always tap into this group and share the channel you have created with them. No matter what your channel is about, there is bound to be at least a few of them who are interested in checking out your videos. Some will want to look up your channel just because of the novelty of one of their co-workers trying to make it big on the video hosting platform. Many content creators don't like to tap into this potential viewer base because they are afraid of how their co-workers will receive their channel, and this type of mindset is understandable, but it needs to be overcome if you want to find success. Being successful in a highly competitive field such as YouTube requires that you use every resource and take every opportunity available in order to maximize the chance of finding an audience and growing.

If the field you currently work in requires a physical business card, this offers another great opportunity to market your YouTube channel. Place the link to your channel, or add your YouTube channel's name, at the bottom of your business card below your contact information. The only thing to remember with this type of marketing is that your channel needs to have content that won't negatively affect your business. For example, if you work at a place that requires the highest level of professionalism and your channel contains very provocative and offensive content, you may not want to associate your channel with your business life. It is very possible that your boss will find out about the content of your channel and they might deem it necessary to fire you. If the channel you have on YouTube is for your job, however, there will be no conflict of interest and you should feel completely safe connecting these two worlds.

Beyond business associates, if you are an individual trying to grow your channel, you might take advantage of the kindness of your friends and relatives once again. This is the best option to get people to check out your channel many times when you are starting out. No one is more likely to take time out of their life to give your YouTube channel a look than someone who is related to you or with whom you are close friends. Even if your content is subpar, they will probably offer positive and constructive criticism that will help you going forward. Friends and family are the most common source of hope for content creators and remain a good option for anyone starting out to get easy views and some positive reinforcement.

Another more extreme tactic utilized in the past is using your car to promote your YouTube channel. This mostly happens if you have a business vehicle that has an advertisement on it anyway. You could very easily add your YouTube username to this mobile advertisement, and instantly everyone in traffic will have the opportunity to view your YouTube channel and check out your content. The odds of people actually looking up the YouTube channel of someone they just ran across in traffic is unlikely, but if only one person out of a hundred does it, you've still created one more potential subscriber without having to do any extra work. While this is usually done by people with business vehicles, it would also be possible to do it with your personal vehicle if you are really serious about growing your channel and want to take things to another level. This would probably require a little money to go to a shop that could create something to put on your car, but the investment might be worth it if you spend a lot of time driving your car each day. You could also add the YouTube username to your car's windshield yourself with some type of permanent marker, but this will likely look unprofessional and may not accomplish anything more than making your car look trashy.

Have Patience

Recently, YouTube made some changes to the way that content creators are able to make money on the video hosting site and this changes things for channels just starting out. First of all, it was never easy when you were first starting out to make money on YouTube. The amount of money that content creators received from the revenue generated from their videos was minuscule and barely worth the effort at times. This was certainly the case when you were first starting out and had not generated a following of any kind on your channel as yet. It was very common that until you were marginally successful, you would not hit the threshold required to even receive a payment of the revenue made on your videos. So having to be patient when it comes to making money on the site is definitely nothing new; however, the recent changes made to the site make it even more important. YouTube recently added new and more extreme qualifications necessary before you are allowed to make any money on the videos hosted on the site. You must have at least one thousand subscribers and receive a large amount of hours viewed on your videos each month to qualify for making money on the website.

This will mean that when you are starting out on the platform and just trying to grow your channel, now more than ever, you will have to be patient and not expect to get any money from your channel for quite some time. The two qualifications together make it nearly impossible to get paid without truly being successful already. The subscriber threshold can easily be surpassed by joining groups on Facebook or Twitter that offer follow type of services, but it still doesn't get you the necessary view time required to make money. This also makes it increasingly difficult to make money if you spend a significant amount of time making each video. The amount of views a video gets always goes down after the video has been posted for a while. For example, a video may get fifty views the first day it is posted and then the next day it will receive thirty-five. The day after, it may receive only twenty. This will go on until your video will only get more views when a new subscriber finds your channel and decides to check out the old content. What this means is that if you spend two weeks or longer making each video, it will more difficult than ever, when you are starting out, to get the number of views necessary to reach the requirement to monetize your videos. Essentially, you will be putting more of an investment in each video, since you will need to obtain more views from each one.

These new requirements may not be permanent, but it is likely that they will be and anyone starting their channel on YouTube should expect it to be the new rules going forward. If you are an hoping to start a career on YouTube, certainly with these new rules in place, you will want to keep your regular job until you have already gained a significant following on the site because you won't be making money starting out. This further establishes that, although you should treat YouTube like a job with the amount of effort you put into it, perhaps when you are starting out, it needs to be treated more as a part-time job than one that you would spend forty hours a week working at.

Work Hard

Everything mentioned in this book has one thing in common: it won't work if you don't put enough effort into it. You may know and believe that you need to make your videos look professional, but how hard are you willing to work and how much are you willing to learn in order to make sure it happens for every video? You may understand that collaborating with other content creators would significantly help your channel, but how much effort reaching out to peers are you willing to give? Every single thing possible to do that can help grow your channel will not work if you don't work hard at it and stick to it for a long period of time. Rarely does success come easy on YouTube these days and you won't find success if you are not willing to put work and time into it every day. YouTube is fantastic because your success really is up to you, but this can also be the downside of it if you aren't motivated enough. The amount of growth you see on YouTube will be directly related to the amount of effort you put into it. Yes, talent and resources, as with anything in life, can play a role; but if you are truly dedicated and exert yourself for your channel and stick to consistently doing the things mentioned in this book, you will inevitably find success.

There will be times when you want to take some time off from working on your channel and step away. This is understandable and perfectly normal, but not recommended in the early phases if you want it to grow to something truly large. In fact, you should treat your time on YouTube as a job of sorts. You should be working on something related to your channel for at least a couple hours every day, if you have a full-time job unrelated to the channel. Looking at YouTube at least in the beginning as a part-time job is the most recommended attitude to have. If your dream is to turn YouTube into a career, maybe down the line you can treat your channel like a full-time job, but at the very least, you should be working on it about ten hours a week. This is the amount of work required in today's digital landscape to be fruitful on YouTube. Hard work is really the only way to guarantee success on the site and it is easily the most important tip that anyone can give to someone interested in growing on the site.

This is the method that will reap a gradual and stable growth of your channel. Instead of the temporary hype that comes with a viral video, slow and gradual growth is actually more valuable. Slowly gaining followers who will stick with you permanently is what you want, and working hard will get you this type of follower. The rare people who hit the lottery and get lucky on YouTube are those who struggle to sustain success. Work hard and watch growth happen.

Make a New Way

No one has all of the answers in this world and there is no doubt that a way not listed here could be great for building a YouTube channel from the ground up. Whether it is something that just got left out of this book, or something never been thought of before, there is certainly something else out there that could help you carve your way into Internet history. The greatest people in the history of the world dared to think outside the box and came up with their own way to the future, so feel free to try different methods that you come up with yourself to grow your YouTube channel. While people have been making channels and videos on YouTube for many years now, at this point, the site and even the Internet itself, is still fairly new, which means that there is still plenty of opportunity for new ideas to sweep in and change the game. The worst thing that can happen is that you fail, but you can learn from that failure. It is, in fact, the most common and organic way to learning how to do something well, and there is nothing wrong with doing YouTube that way, too. Failure will be a constant when you are working on YouTube. Even if you have a track record of creating content that users enjoy, there will be a video every now and then that fails to connect with your audience. So, understanding failure can be as valuable as you grow your channel as not getting discouraged by things when they happen. It is all a learning process.

If you are putting thought into different and new ways to grow, it means that you are putting in the work and will definitely find success. So keep at it and think outside the box, as this is the way to find a new and unique way to...

Make Some Noise

YouTube is easily the most popular video sharing website in the world. The traffic it gets on a daily basis is through the roof compared to smaller and similar sites like Vimeo or Dailymotion. The fact that so many people go to YouTube to watch videos on the Internet, whether it's a viral video everyone is talking about or a guy playing a video game for half an hour, makes having a popular channel really enticing. YouTube is the place that makes people into stars these days in entertainment; it is no longer just television and movies. In fact, YouTube stars have landed television and movie deals in the past, due to their popularity on the website. Some have been able to create profitable careers out of being comedians after starting out on YouTube. Businesses, and rightfully so, see YouTube as a huge opportunity to reach potential clients and customers and have flocked to the site to advertise their services. There is something for everyone on the website which this is why so many people want to grow their channel to begin with. The issue, of course, is that since everyone wants to have a popular channel on YouTube, how is it possible for this to happen when the site is so densely populated with different people creating content and building channels. Is there enough room on the site for everyone? Are there enough viewers out there for everyone to find an audience and grow their channel up to millions of subscribers?

There does seem to be, but it is no longer easy to build a channel up to popularity because it is so crowded. Now the only way to find an audience and succeed on the site is to work extremely hard. Make videos that look professional. Be consistent about when you post and learn to build relationships. Work well with other content creators and give back to your subscribers on a regular basis. Be prepared to capitalize on a viral video that may come from your channel and learn to use SEO in your video tags. All these tips will help you compete in a cutthroat and difficult-to-break-through platform like YouTube. Whether you are an individual just trying to make a career for yourself, or are a part of a business trying to add revenue, creativity is one of the most important ingredients for success on YouTube. Be creative in the way you market yourself and your channel, or your business and your channel. Take advantage of every possible way you can think of to gain subscribers and viewers. Keep in mind that every common way to build a channel is probably being done by everyone else trying to make a successful YouTube channel, and realize that you need to do all of these things plus more than that as well. The only things that separate your channel from everybody else's is the hard work you put into it and the creativity you employ to find a way to put your channel out there.

Conclusion

I hope this book was able to help you to point out important steps and techniques to improve your youtube channel and help you find ways to gain new subscribers. Now it's on you to take **massive action** and put in even more work and effort than ever before!

If you liked this book, I would highly appreciate if you could leave a review on Amazon!

On the following pages you'll find a free excerpt of my book "Facebook Marketing Guide".

Bonus Chapter: Understanding Facebook Marketing

Facebook is one of the largest social network platforms in the world with at least more than 1.30 billion active users, meaning that about 62% of users log into Facebook daily, a fact that makes it such a dynamic marketing platform. According to eMarketer, about 41% of US small businesses use Facebook as part of their online marketing strategy. The momentum with which Facebook has grown right from its launch a few years ago to where it is today only shows that it will likely experience continual growth in the future. Having such a large user base makes it a great selling platform, and ignoring it isn't an option for serious marketers.

Even with the widespread use of Facebook for marketing purposes, only about 45% of business owners have reported success with their Facebook marketing efforts, according to a survey carried out by Social Media Examiner. Business owners therefore need to understand the strategies and practices capable of granting them a positive return on investment that's worth the effort. Understanding the major components of Facebook marketing is vital to equip business owners with best practices and actionable insights that, if properly implemented, have the potential of giving the desired results.

Every day, Facebook presents entrepreneurs with a market for their products and services, and the question arises as to how one can target such a huge user base. Facebook has made it easy for marketers to establish an advertising platform and specify the type of people they want to target with their strategies. Marketers can target the right market using location of users, as well as interests and demographics. Understanding how you can use Facebook marketing to your advantage is quite vital for the success of a business.

Facebook started as a social network platform for college students, but has so far evolved into a platform that anyone with an Internet connection can access. The minimum age required for users is just 13 years, which covers a wide base of users, and it is being used by people of all ages. Facebook is popularly used by those between 18 and 65; however, the above and below age groups tend to minimally engage with the platform. Regardless of the age group you're targeting, you will find more than enough users to interact with on Facebook.

- Engaging in Facebook marketing can help you realize may things:
- Strengthen brand identity
- Collect feedback from customers and build customer relationships
- Direct customers to your website

- Ability to be found by those looking for your products
- Create targeted advertising for promoting your business
- Generate word of mouth advertising
- Establish and demonstrate your expertise

How to Market on Facebook

There are three tools that marketers can use for marketing on Facebook. These tools are Facebook pages, Facebook ads and Facebook Groups. Each of the tools has a way to be used and often varies; however, all can be used together for greater reach of the targeted market.

Pages

Facebook page is similar to a profile; however, it's mostly used by organizations, businesses and public figures. Users get to "like" the page which then automatically enables them to receive updates from it into their newsfeeds. Unlike profiles that require mutual friendships, pages can be liked by anybody. Pages also don't have any restriction on the number of people who can like the page unlike profiles that are limited to 5,000 people. Pages are quite easy to set up; bu7t building a fun base or a team of committed customers can be quite a challenge.

Ads

This is a targeted advertising platform marketers can use to create ads that target specific geographic areas; they can be filtered in terms of education levels, age and the type of devices used for browsing. Users are free to close ads they don't like and can "like" the page just below the advertisement. Ads are designed with powerful parameters that are quite ideal for targeting: the only downside is that they can be a bit expensive depending on one's goal.

Groups

Facebook groups are akin to discussion forums but have additional features similar to profiles and pages. You can create a group related to your area of business or industry, enabling you to connect with potential customers. Groups are free to use and allow for high levels of engagement. The challenge is that they can be quite time consuming.

There are various marketing strategies that can be used on Facebook; however, focusing on what is less expensive has the potential of bringing greater returns and is thus quite beneficial for business purposes. Inbound marketing is one of the ways that tends to yield great returns if well executed. It entails engaging with your audience in a way they find relatable and helpful. It involves getting to know customer goals and collaborating with them as you help them overcome the challenges they face. The best way to execute this strategy is by being available where your audience spends time - which is Facebook.

The tools available for marketers on Facebook cater to those willing to form relationships with their audience. Marketers should be able to create and distribute content that their audience finds valuable and helpful. Quality content enables marketers to connect with consumers interested in the services offered or their brands. Pushing content that your audience is not interested in can be perceived as annoying, spammy or even deceiving. Facebook marketing requires a long-term commitment and consistency in delivering quality content.

To succeed in Facebook marketing, one should clearly distinguish between Facebook advertising and Facebook marketing. As much as your Facebook marketing strategy may incorporate Facebook advertising, your strategy should also involve building engaging and lasting relationships with your audience. The content you share should not always be geared towards making a sale or pitching a product; connecting and providing helpful information to your social network can go a long way toward providing long-term reliable customers you can engage with.

You don't need a big budget to get started and be successful at Facebook marketing; commitment to providing valuable content in a reliable and consistent way can greatly help in connecting with potential customers and fans. All you have to do as you start out is to ensure that you highlight your brand values in a clear and effective way, identify your audience and their demographics, while also creating a unique space for your company. Remember that when it comes to Facebook marketing, sometimes the simplest form of communication can be the most powerful.

If you have a product or service that's considered to be boring, you can awe your audience by incorporating beautiful images to highlight the creative side of your brand. Take advantage of the virtual reality features provided on Facebook to enhance your content.

Developing a Facebook Marketing Strategy

Starting off with your Facebook marketing plan without having a clear strategy in place can only lead to failure, as you're likely to become overwhelmed in the process. Take time and define your marketing strategy; just going ahead and starting a Facebook page without a clear strategy may not grant you the desired results. You should have a clear strategy on how to meet your business goals and get the most out of every investment you make on Facebook. Below are some of the strategies you can consider putting in place.

Define your Audience

Targeting the right audience effectively may not be possible if you don't know your audience well. Defining it may not be easy if you're just starting out; however, an overview of Facebook demographics and having brand intelligence about the customer profile will act as the first building block in developing an understanding of how your audience may turn out to be. You can use tools such as

Facebook audience insights to investigate key details about potential customers you may find on Facebook. Details such as age, gender, relationship status, education, location, Facebook usage and past purchase activity can give you insight into how to define your audience.

Set your Goals

Having clear marketing goals is also vital. You can invest in getting more "likes" to your business page; but if the likes are not part of your broader marketing plan, then having more likes may not yield great returns. Remember the goals differ from one business to another but should be based on specific actions that will have an impact on the bottom line, actions that lead to increased conversions to your website, generating leads and improving customer service response. These may be broad marketing goals, and you can consider goals that are more specific and measurable.

Every engagement you involve yourself in, whether it is posting content, making a comment or even designing an ad, should support your business goals. You can instill all the aspects of your Facebook marketing plan by having a marketing mission statement that suits your brand. It should enable you to maintain a brand voice that is consistent in all your Facebook marketing activities. Having a goal gives the marketing process direction and is a way of measuring the success. Some of the business goals for using Facebook include:

- Find people searching for the services or products you are offering
- Connect and engage with potential and current customers
- Build a community around your business
- Promote your other content such as webinars, blog articles and the like

Create a Facebook Marketing Plan

Once you have set goals, you will then develop a clear plan on how to achieve them. One vital plan you should formulate is determining the ideal content mix for your audience. You can follow the common 80 – 20 rule. This is where 80 percent of your Facebook posts are focused on informing, educating and entertaining with the other 20 percent focused on directly promoting your brand. The key thing about Facebook you need to remember is that the engagements should be geared towards relationships, and the constant pitching of your products may not be the best way to build them.

If you're committed to providing valuable content that your followers find helpful and keeps them engaged, they will be open learning about the services or products you are offering with the 20 percent of the sales-focused posts. You can also follow the social media rule of thirds to provide a mix of promotional posts and valuable content. It entails a third of your content covering ideas and stories, a third involving personal interactions with your followers, and the remaining one-third focused on promoting your business. Regardless of the plan you choose, it should be aimed at providing more valuable content than promotional material so as to keep your audience engaged and interested.

According to Facebook algorithms, brands that focus more on driving sales often get penalized. Facebook require that users' feeds be filled with content they like and are willing to share instead of sales pitches. Remember that likes and shares help extend your reach as they puts your brand before many people without any direct effort from your side.

After defining your content mix, the next step is to determine how frequently you should post. As much as posts don't appear in their chronological order based on the algorithms, you can plan on posting at a time when your audience is more active on the platform. Establish a content calendar to help with balancing and mixing different types of content for your posting to be on track.

27889884R00042

Printed in Great Britain
by Amazon